NO PART OF THIS BOOK MAY BE USED OR REPRODUCED IN ANY MANNER
WITHOUT WRITTEN PERMISSION. EXCEPT IN THE CASE OF BRIEF QUOTATIONS
EMBODIED IN CRITICAL ARTICLES OR REVIEWS.
FOR MORE INFORMATION CONTACT,
R.B. MOSBY
BMOSBY111@GMAIL.COM
VANCOUVER B.C.
CANADA
"THINGS I WOULD SAY TO FIVE YEAR OLD ME"
(A BOOK OF LIFE LESSONS FOR EVERYONE)
COPYRIGHT © 2024
BY R.B. MOSBY
BRITISH COLUMBIA, CANADA
ALL RIGHTS RESERVED

TO:

FROM:

DISCLAIMER...
"THINGS I WOULD SAY TO FIVE YEAR OLD ME"
IS FOR EVERYONE,
NO MATTER YOUR AGE OR GENDER.
THE CONVERSATION BEING HAD IS BETWEEN MYSELF AND
YOUNGER ME,
A MAN TO A BOY, BUT IT PERTAINS TO EVERYONE, IT
PERTAINS TO LIFE IN GENERAL
AND IS NOT MEANT TO
EXCLUDE ANYONE IN ANY WAY...
ENJOY!!!

THIS BOOK IS DEDICATED TO
MY FAMILY,
MY FATHER AND MOTHER
AND HUGE BABY BROTHER.
TO LESLIE, THE JUICE,
BENNY, CINDY,
GLENN AND FAMILY, AND
ALL THE FRIENDS I'VE MADE
ON THIS CRAZY JOURNEY...
(YOU ALL SHOULD KNOW
WHO YOU ARE)

It all started with
what I thought was a simple question...
"What would you say to five year old you"
Admittedly shocked,
when I realized simple it was not,
I wasn't quite sure what to do...

Then it hit me like a flash,
and I smiled and I could see,
so many things that I would say to
young five year old me...

I found myself writing,
so many different things,
about lessons not often taught,
and the hardships this world brings.

IT BECAME A CONVERSATION,
I WOULD HAVE WITH MY MUCH YOUNGER SELF.
AND THROUGH THAT, BECAME A REMINDER,
THAT WE SHOULD ALWAYS BELIEVE IN
OURSELVES.

I HOPE YOU ALL ENJOY THESE PAGES,
AND THAT YOU'LL READ THEM ALL THE WAY THROUGH,
AND WITH THAT, NOW I'D LIKE TO ASK YOU THE SAME QUESTION...
WHAT WOULD YOU SAY TO FIVE YEAR OLD YOU?

AND
THE
CONVERSATION
BEGINS...

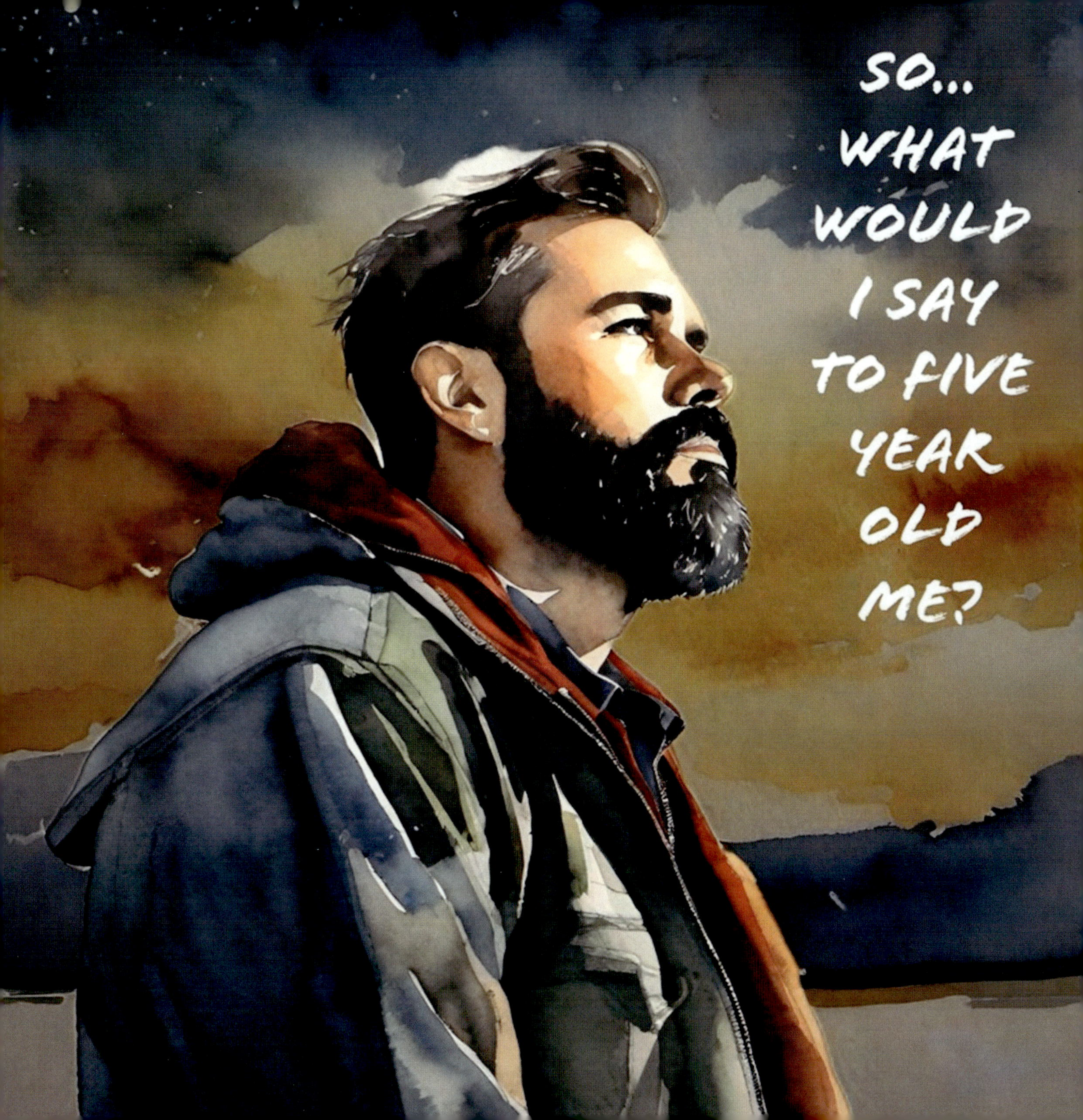
SO...
WHAT
WOULD
I SAY
TO FIVE
YEAR
OLD
ME?

WELL...
I'D SAY THAT THIS LIFE,
IS LIKE THE RINGS OF A
TREE...

THIS MAY BE A LITTLE HARD
TO UNDERSTAND,
AS YOU ARE STILL JUST SMALL,
BUT I'LL DO MY BEST TO
EXPLAIN SOME THINGS TO YOU,
GOOD, BAD, AND ALL...

ON THE INSIDE OF ALL OF THE TREES YOU SEE, THERE ARE MANY DIFFERENT LAYERS.

AND JUST LIKE YOU, THEY WILL CHANGE AS THEY GROW, THROUGHOUT ALL THEIR LIVING YEARS...

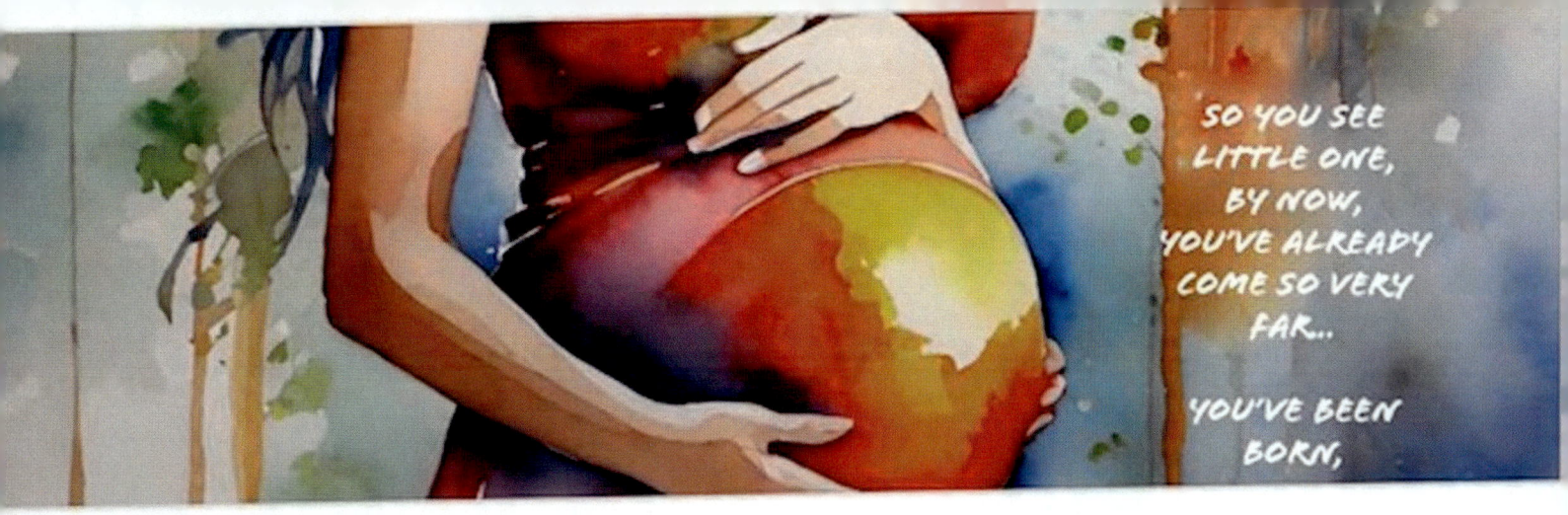

So you see little one, by now, you've already come so very far...

You've been born,

and you've grown,

and now, here you are!

AT THIS POINT IN YOUR LIFE, YOU ALREADY KNOW MORE, THAN YOU COULD POSSIBLY UNDERSTAND...

AND IF YOU'LL JUST LISTEN CLOSELY, YOU'LL GROW INTO AN AMAZING MAN...

I MUST TELL YOU THOUGH, THIS GROWTH WILL BE TOUGH, SOME DAYS YOU'LL SUCCEED, AND SOME DAYS YOU WILL FAIL, AND SOME DAYS YOU WONT FEEL LIKE YOU'RE ENOUGH...

BUT YOU WILL ALWAYS BE ENOUGH, AND YOU ARE HERE FOR A REASON...

JUST LIKE EVERY SINGLE TREE,

STANDING THROUGH EVERY SINGLE SEASON.

You started out just like any tree, just as small as can be, you're growing bigger every day, and you're learning in every way.

This first lesson is to tell you, pay attention to everything you'll see, and one day soon you'll realize, all the things that you could be...

AND JUST LIKE EVERY TREE, YOU'LL STAND THROUGH ALL KINDS OF WEATHER...

OUR WORLD CAN SHOW US THE SCARIEST OF THINGS!

BUT IF YOU ARE HONEST AND TRUE, AND ALWAYS TRY TO BE YOUR BEST YOU,

YOU'LL BE ROOTED AND STRONG FOR WHATEVER THIS CRAZY WORLD BRINGS...

GOOD CHOICES...

BAD CHOICES...

THIS WORLD WILL BRING YOU CHOICES, AND CONSEQUENCES FOR THE THINGS YOU DO, WITH EACH CHOICE YOU'LL HAVE TWO DOORS TO CHOOSE FROM, CHOOSE THE ONE THAT FEELS RIGHT TO YOU...

AND YOU'LL CHOOSE THE WRONG DOOR, MANY, MANY DIFFERENT TIMES, BUT WHEN YOU YOU CHOOSE THE RIGHT ONE, IT'S BEHIND THIS ONE YOU'LL FIND...

THAT THE BEAUTY, AND LOVE, AND THE KINDNESS YOU'LL SEE, WILL FAR OUTWEIGH THE BAD, THAT THIS WORLD CAN SOMETIMES BE.

SO WHAT I'M SAYING WITH THIS, AND I HOPE YOU UNDERSTAND, IS THAT THIS LIFE WILL BE DIFFICULT, BUT IT WILL RARELY BE BLAND...

YOU WILL FIND LOVE, AND YOU'LL LOSE IT...

YOU'LL LOSE LOVED ONES, BUT YOU'LL LIVE THROUGH IT...

YOU'LL WONDER WHY ANYTHING BAD COULD EVER HAPPEN TO YOU, AND YOU'LL WONDER WHY THIS WORLD WOULD TAKE PEOPLE AWAY FROM YOU...

WELL, TO THAT I CAN ONLY SAY THIS...

OUR WORLD CAN BE UNFAIR,
AND IT WILL ALWAYS KEEP YOU GUESSING,
SO TREAT EVERY MOMENT LIKE IT'S A MIRACLE,
AND TREAT EVERY DAY LIKE IT'S A BLESSING!

YOU'LL GROW UP AROUND OTHER KIDS, THAT SEEM TO THINK THEY'RE BETTER THAN YOU, BUT JUST KEEP LISTENING CLOSELY, I'VE GOT A FEW MORE THINGS TO TELL YOU...

YOU'LL NEED TO BE STRONG AS YOU GROW,
AND ALWAYS STAND UP FOR YOURSELF,
FEED THE LION IN YOU, NOT THE LAMB,
AND NEVER LEAVE YOUR DREAMS ON A SHELF...

DO NOT TRY TO BE PERFECT, DO NOT EVEN TRY TO TRY, AS YOU WILL NEVER HAVE TO BE, AND HERE'S THE REASON WHY...

YOU SEE NOBODY IS PERFECT, AS MUCH AS THEY SEEM TO BE, BUT YOU ARE PERFECTLY IMPERFECT, JUST LIKE EVERY PERFECT TREE...

YOU'LL MAKE FRIENDS AS YOU GO...

AND MAKE SOME ENEMIES TOO...

AND MEET MANY DIFFERENT PEOPLE, VERY DIFFERENT FROM YOU...

SO BE RESPECTFUL AND ACCEPTING WHEN
YOU MEET SOMEONE NEW,
OR YOU'LL NEVER KNOW THE JOY IN
MEETING PEOPLE DIFFERENT FROM YOU...

AND STAY TRUE TO YOUR FRIENDS, THEY'LL BECOME YOUR FAMILY LATER ON...

THEY WILL HELP YOU FACE YOUR ENEMIES,
SO YOU CAN TAKE THEM HEAD ON...

THIS LIFE OF OURS IS AN UPHILL CLIMB, WITH MANY STEPS ALONG THE WAY, AND YOU ARE BOUND TO FIND A VARIETY OF STRUGGLES, WITHIN EVERY SINGLE DAY...

BUT THERE IS A SAMENESS IN OUR STRUGGLES,
AS WE'RE ALL LIVING THE SAME GAME,
AND YOU'LL NOTICE MORE AS YOU GROW,
EVERYONE SMILES AND CRIES THE SAME.

YOU'LL SEE OTHER PEOPLE LIVES THAT SEEM BETTER THAN YOURS,

WITH SO MANY MORE OPTIONS, AND SO MUCH MORE IN STORE.

BUT THIS IS NOT THE CASE, EVERYONE TRIES AND EVERYONE FAILS, BUT THE QUESTION IS, WILL YOU LEARN FROM YOUR MISTAKES, AND RESET THOSE LITTLE SAILS?

THE ANSWER
SHOULD ALWAYS
BE YES!
AND EVEN THEN
YOU CAN STILL
FEEL STUCK,
BUT ALWAYS
REMEMBER TO
KEEP FIGHTING
YOUR WAY OUT
OF THIS LIFE'S
MUCK...

AND IF YOU DO FIND, THAT YOU NEED TO FIGHT, ONLY DO IT IF YOU HAVE TO, AND ONLY DO IT TO PROTECT YOURSELF, AND THE LOVED ONES AROUND YOU!

YOU'RE PROBABLY STARTING TO UNDERSTAND, THAT THIS LIFE WILL BE HARD, AND THERE WILL UNDOUBTEDLY BE TIMES, THAT WILL LEAVE YOU SCARRED...

BUT IF YOU LEARN FROM THESE LESSONS, AND STAY STRONG ON YOUR JOURNEY, YOU'LL GROW UP TO BE A BETTER PERSON, THAN YOU EVER KNEW YOU COULD BE...

AND THERE WILL STILL BE MANY DAYS,
WHEN YOU FEEL YOU JUST CAN'T STAND THE WEATHER...
BUT YOU'LL LEARN YOU'RE NOT THE ONLY ONE,
AS WE ALL LEARN THIS LIFE TOGETHER...

So, be kindhearted and considerate, to all those around you, especially to your parents, as they're the reason this world has found you...

THEY'VE HAD STRUGGLES OF THEIR OWN, AND THEY'RE NOT PERFECT YOU SEE, AND MAYBE IT'S BECAUSE NOBODY TOLD THEM, THEY ARE AS STRONG AS A TREE

CAN I COME OUT NOW? I'M BEING-HAVED!
AND YOU MUST UNDERSTAND, THEY ARE STILL LEARNING TOO, AND SOME DAYS IT WILL FEEL LIKE THEIR LOVE DOESN'T SURROUND YOU...

But remember that it's there, and it always will be, and with their help, you'll grow as big and strong, as the biggest, strongest tree...

AND THEN MAYBE ONE DAY,
THERE MAY COME ANOTHER,
ANOTHER LITTLE SPROUT,
MAYBE A SISTER OR BROTHER...

AND LIKE YOU,
THEY WILL
GROW,
AND THEY'LL
LEARN
AND THEY'LL
SEE,
ALL THE VALUE
AND THE
STRENGTH
IN THE PERSON
THEY CAN BE...

THEIR STRUGGLES AND SUCCESSES WILL BE DIFFERENT FROM YOURS...

THERE WILL EVEN BE TIMES, WHEN IT SEEMS THE WORLD LOVES THEM MORE...

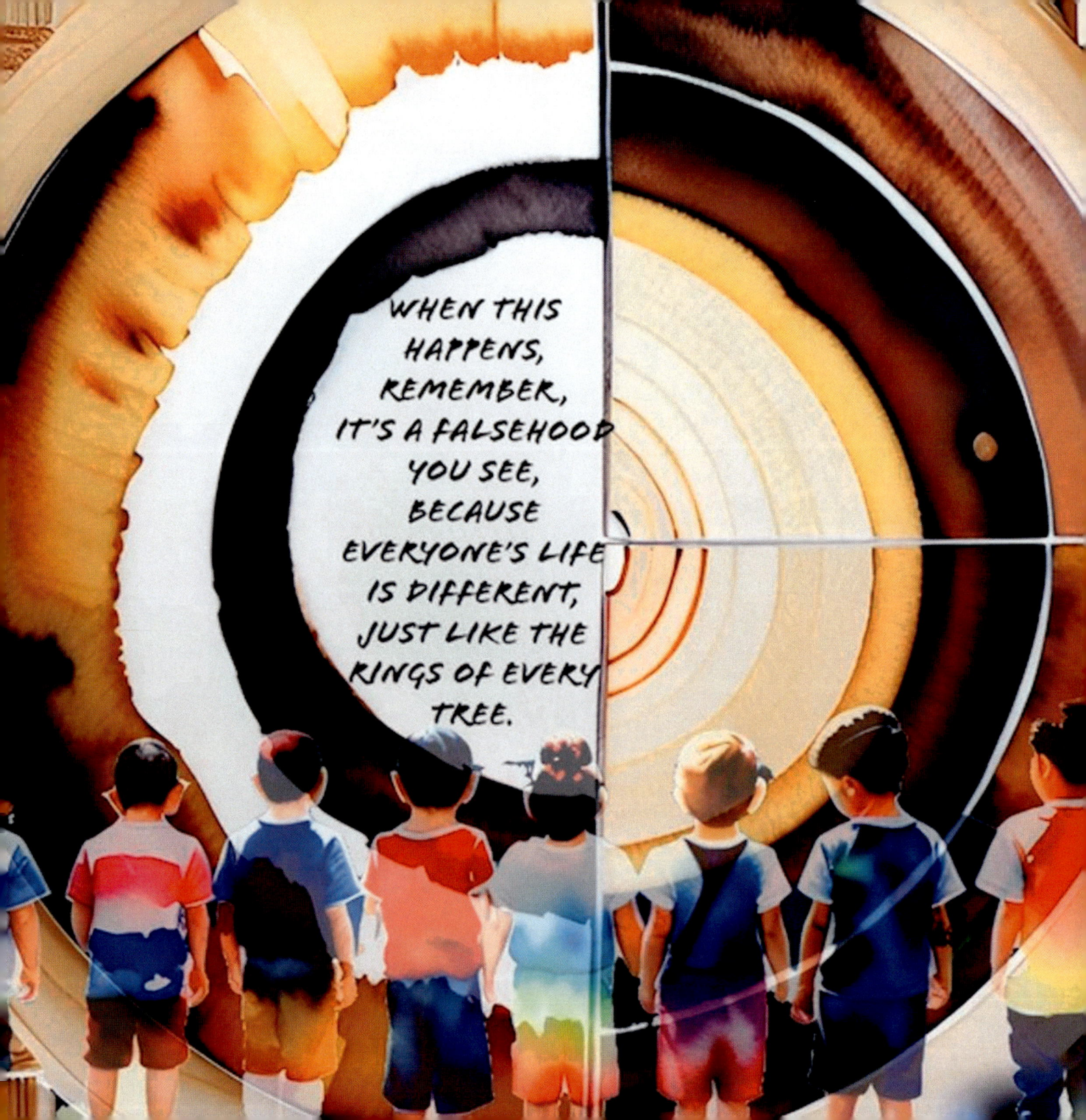

WHEN THIS HAPPENS, REMEMBER, IT'S A FALSEHOOD YOU SEE, BECAUSE EVERYONE'S LIFE IS DIFFERENT, JUST LIKE THE RINGS OF EVERY TREE.

YOU WILL BE DIFFERENT FROM EACH OTHER, YOUR LITTLE SISTER OR BROTHER, YOU WILL LOVE THEM AND TEACH THEM AND PROTECT THEM IN KIND,

AND THEY WILL LOVE YOU AND TEACH YOU, AND ONE DAY YOU'LL FIND...

THAT YOU WILL DO YOUR
BEST TO HELP THEM,
TO FIND THEIR OWN WAY,
AND YOU'LL DO YOUR
BEST TO SHELTER THEM,
ON ANY A RAINY DAY....

BUT THERE WILL BE SUNNY DAYS TOO,
THAT YOU WILL SPEND TOGETHER,
JUST LIKE TWO TREES STANDING STRONG,
NO MATTER WHAT THE WEATHER.

NOW, THIS IS NOT TO SAY,
THAT EVERY DAY WILL BE EASY,
AND JUST LIKE TWO TREES,
YOU'LL BOTH BEND WHEN IT'S BREEZY.

AND THERE WILL ALWAYS SEEM TO BE, MANY STRUGGLES ABOUND, AS OUR PARENTS WILL ALWAYS BE LEARNING HOW TO LIVE WITH US AROUND...

SO TRY TO FOCUS ON THE GOOD THINGS, NOT THE BAD
IN YOUR FAMILY,
BECAUSE OUR FAMILIES HAVE LAYERS TOO,
JUST LIKE THE RINGS OF ANY TREE.

So, a question you may ask is...
How do we see, the inside and growth of the rings of a tree?

Do we have to cut it down? You may ask innocently, well, the answer is yes, as sad as it may be.

BUT THIS LIFE CAN BE HARD, AS I HAVE SAID BEFORE, SOME TREES MAKE IT AND SOME WON'T, SOME OF US GET TO LIVE LONG LIVES AND SOME OF US DON'T...

AND YOU SEE, WITHOUT THE SACRIFICE OF SO MANY TREES, WE WOULD HAVE SO MANY FEWER THINGS THAN SO MANY THINGS YOU'LL SEE...

LIKE MOST HOUSES,
OR A TABLE,
LIKE A BASEBALL BAT,
OR A FABLE WRITTEN
IN THE BOOKS
WE READ JUST TO HELP
US FIND OUR WAY,
AND THE FRAMES OF
THE DOORS WE WALK
THROUGH, EVERY
SINGLE DAY...

THIS LESSON IS TO TELL YOU TO ALWAYS
BE RESPECTFUL OF THIS AMAZING WORLD THAT SURROUNDS YOU,
EVERY LEAF ON EVERY TREE, AND EVERY CREATURE THAT YOU SEE,
HAS THE SAME RIGHT TO BE HERE AS YOU DO.

BUT IN THE SAME BREATH, WE ALL NEED TO EAT, WHETHER IT'S TREES THAT FEED ON SUNSHINE OR LIONS THAT FEED ON MEAT. NEVER, EVER BE WASTEFUL WITH THE GIFTS OUR WORLD HAS TO GIVE, OUR WORLD'S RESOURCES ARE LIMITED, BUT WE ALL NEED THEM TO LIVE...

As the years start to go by, you're going to grow so much more, you'll be looking through wiser eyes, but you might be feeling a bit worn...

So, at the start of each new day,
get yourself out and about,
some things wont go your way,
do your best not to pout.

And life will knock you down, more and more and more, but each time you're brave enough to pick yourself up, you'll be strengthening that little core!

YOU'LL BE LEARNING SO MANY LESSONS, THAT THIS LIFE WILL PROVIDE, ALWAYS TRY TO STAY POSITIVE, ALWAYS TRY TO STAY IN STRIDE...

TRY TO FOCUS ON THE BEAUTIFUL THINGS,
NOT THE UGLINESS YOU'LL SEE,
OUR WORLD CAN BE A HARD PLACE TO LIVE,
BUT LIVING A GOOD LIFE CAN BE EASY...

MAKE YOUR BED EVERY DAY, LEARN FROM YOUR MISTAKES, AND NEVER STEAL, CHEAT OR LIE, ALWAYS DO YOUR BEST, TRY TO LIVE OUT YOUR DREAMS, AND ALWAYS REACH FOR THE SKY!

THERE IS ONLY ONE FINISH LINE, IN THIS CRAZY LIFE OF YOURS AND MINE, SO MAKE THE MOST OF IT I ASK YOU PLEASE, CLIMB EVERY MOUNTAIN AND SAIL ALL THE SEAS...

I HOPE THAT THESE LESSONS AREN'T TOO HARD TO UNDERSTAND, AND I HOPE YOU READ THEM OVER AND OVER, AS YOU GROW INTO A YOUNG MAN...

YOU ARE GOING TO DO GREAT THINGS LITTLE ONE,
THIS I CAN SURELY SEE,
AND EVERYDAY YOU'LL GET JUST A LITTLE BIT CLOSER,
TO THIS MESSAGE FROM ME...

THAT YOUR LIFE, WILL BE JUST LIKE, THE RINGS OF A TREE...

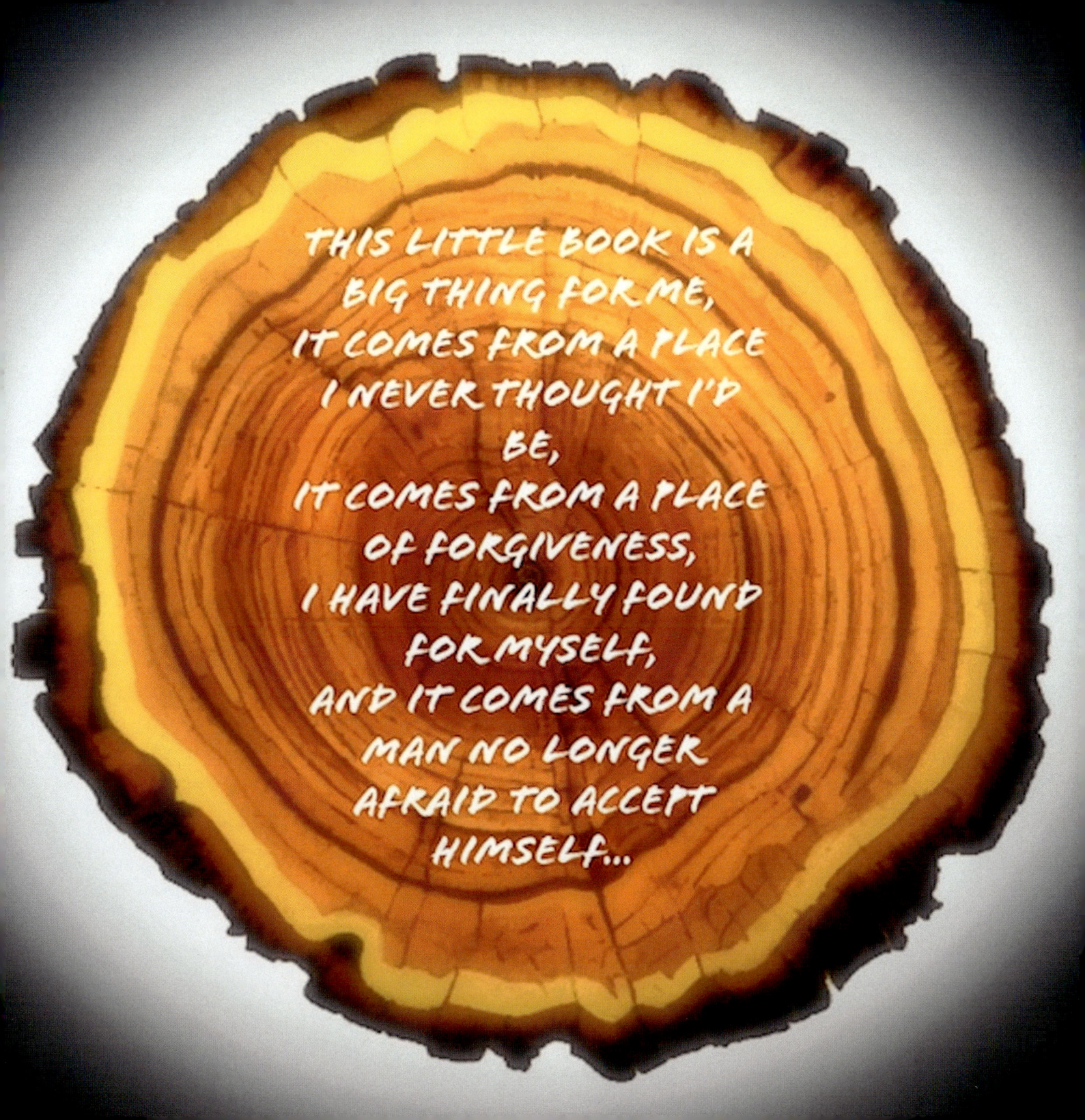

This little book is a big thing for me,
It comes from a place I never thought I'd be,
It comes from a place of forgiveness,
I have finally found for myself,
And it comes from a man no longer afraid to accept himself...

Manufactured by Amazon.ca
Bolton, ON